The Heritage Collection

Volume Two

★

The Best Loved Songs of the American Stage

★

AMERICAN REVOLUTION BICENTENNIAL

1776-1976

OFFICIALLY RECOGNIZED
COMMEMORATIVE OF THE
AMERICAN REVOLUTION
BICENTENNIAL
ADMINISTRATION

D0074369

License No. 76-19-0556
Authorized Under
Public Law 93-179

Produced by Murray Sporn & John Dentato
for The Song Book Company.

From "PROMISES, PROMISES"

I'LL NEVER FALL IN LOVE AGAIN

Lyric by HAL DAVID

Music by BURT BACHARACH

5

6

From: "BELLS ARE RINGING"

LONG BEFORE I KNEW YOU

Words by **BETTY COMDEN**
and **ADOLPH GREEN**

Music by **JULE STYNE**

From "STOP THE WORLD—I WANT TO GET OFF"

GONNA BUILD A MOUNTAIN

Words and Music by
LESLIE BRICUSSE & ANTHONY NEWLEY

Fairly bright tempo

1. Gon-na Build A Moun-tain — From a lit-tle hill.
2. (Gon-na build a) day-dream (Yeah, Yeah,) From a lit-tle hope. (Yeah, Yeah,)
3. (Gon-na build a) heav-en — From a lit-tle hell.

Gon-na Build A Moun-tain — least I hope I will.
Gon-na push that day-dream (Yeah, Yeah,) up the moun-tain slope. (Yeah, Yeah,)
Gon-na build a heav-en — and I know darn well.

EXTRA VERSES

5.

Gonna build a heaven from a little hell
Gonna build a heaven and I know well
With a fine young son who will take my place
There'll be a sun in my heaven on earth
With the good Lord's grace.

6.

Gonna build a mountain from a little hill.
Gonna build a mountain — least I hope I will.
Gonna build a mountain — gonna build it high.
I don't know how I'm gonna do it
I only know I'm gonna try.

From "ONE TOUCH OF VENUS"

SPEAK LOW

Words by **OGDEN NASH**

Music by **KURT WEILL**

From "GIGI"

THANK HEAVEN FOR LITTLE GIRLS

Words by **ALAN JAY LERNER**

Music by **FREDERICK LOEWE**

From: "WISH YOU WERE HERE"

WISH YOU WERE HERE

Words and Music by
HAROLD ROME

Refrain *(in dreamy Beguine tempo)*

They're not mak-ing the skies as blue this year. Wish you were here! As blue as they used to when you were near. Wish you were here! And the morn-ings don't seem as

From "MY FAIR LADY"

WOULDN'T IT BE LOVERLY

Words by **ALAN JAY LERNER**

Music by **FREDERICK LOEWE**

From "KISMET"

STRANGER IN PARADISE

Words and Music by
ROBERT WRIGHT and
GEORGE FORREST

29

From: "KEEPS RAININ' ALL THE TIME"

STORMY WEATHER

(Keeps Rainin' All The Time)

Music by HAROLD ARLEN
Words by TED KOEHLER

From "KISMET"

BAUBLES, BANGLES AND BEADS

Words and Music by
ROBERT WRIGHT and
GEORGE FORREST

sing, sing-a-ling-a, Wear-ing bau-bles, ban-gles and beads. I'll glit-ter and gleam so, Make some-bod-y dream so That some-day he may

From "BORN TO DANCE"

I'VE GOT YOU UNDER MY SKIN

Words and Music by
COLE PORTER

got you _____ un-der my skin. _____ I

tried so _____ not to give in, _____ I

said to my-self,"This af - fair nev-er will go so well." _____ But

why should I try to re - sist when, dar-ling, I know so well _____ I've

From "MY FAIR LADY"

I'VE GROWN ACCUSTOMED TO HER FACE

Words by **ALAN JAY LERNER**

Music by **FREDERICK LOEWE**

From: "DUBARRY WAS A LADY"

DO I LOVE YOU?

Words and Music by
COLE PORTER

From "HELLO, DOLLY!"

IT ONLY TAKES A MOMENT

Words and Music by
JERRY HERMAN

IT'S A BIG WIDE WONDERFUL WORLD

Words and Music by
JOHN ROX

From "I DO, I DO"

MY CUP RUNNETH OVER

Words by **TOM JONES**

Music by **HARVEY SCHMIDT**

From: "GOOD NEWS"

LUCKY IN LOVE

B.G. DeSYLVA, LEW BROWN
and RAY HENDERSON

From "CAN-CAN"

C'EST MAGNIFIQUE

Words and Music by
COLE PORTER

Love is such a fan-tas-tic af-fair when it comes to call. ___ Af-ter tak-ing you up in the air, down it lets you fall. ___ But be pa-tient and

*PRONOUNCE: SAY MAN-YEE-FEE-KUH

soon you will find,   if you fol-low your   heart, not   your mind,

Love   is wait-ing   there a-gain,   to take you up in the

air   a -   gain.

Refrain (*Slow and easy*)

When   love   comes   in   and   takes you   for   a

*Pronounced "say man-yee-fee-kuh"

From "ME AND JULIET"

NO OTHER LOVE

Words by OSCAR HAMMERSTEIN II

Music by RICHARD RODGERS

From: "A DAMSEL IN DISTRESS"

A FOGGY DAY

Words by **IRA GERSHWIN**

Music by **GEORGE GERSHWIN**

I viewed the morn-ing with a-larm,—

The Brit-ish Mu-se — um had lost its charm.—

How long, I won-dered, could this thing last?—

But the age of mir - a-cles had-n't passed,—

From "LES GIRLS"

CA, C'EST L'AMOUR

Words and Music by
COLE PORTER

From "THE MUSIC MAN"

TILL THERE WAS YOU

Words and Music by
MEREDITH WILLSON

From "THE NEW YORKERS"

LOVE FOR SALE

Words and Music by
COLE PORTER

REFRAIN (*with swinging rhythm and not fast*)

Love _____ for sale, _____ Ap-pe-tiz-ing young love for sale._____ Love that's fresh and still un-spoiled, Love that's on-ly slight-ly soiled, Love _____ for sale._____ Who _____ will buy? _____

78

From "OUT OF THIS WORLD"

FROM THIS MOMENT ON

Words and Music by
COLE PORTER

From "SOUTH PACIFIC"

HAPPY TALK

Lyrics by **OSCAR HAMMERSTEIN II**

Music by **RICHARD RODGERS**

From "SHUFFLE ALONG"

I'M JUST WILD ABOUT HARRY

Words by NOBLE SISSLE

Music by EUBIE BLAKE

From "ST. LOUIS WOMAN"

COME RAIN OR COME SHINE

Words by JOHNNY MERCER

Music by HAROLD ARLEN

From: "PORGY AND BESS"

IT AIN'T NECESSARILY SO

Lyrics by **IRA GERSHWIN**

Music by **GEORGE GERSHWIN**

From "WORDS AND MUSIC"

MAD ABOUT THE BOY

Words and Music by
NOEL COWARD

108

From "GUYS AND DOLLS"

LUCK BE A LADY

Words and Music by
FRANK LOESSER

Nev - er get out of my sight_____

Stick with me ba - by I'm the fel - low you came in with,

Luck be a la - dy, luck be a la - dy, Luck be a la - dy to - night.

From "MY FAIR LADY"

ON THE STREET WHERE YOU LIVE

Words by **ALAN JAY LERNER**

Music by **FREDERICK LOEWE**

From: "NO STRINGS"

THE SWEETEST SOUNDS

Words and Music by
RICHARD RODGERS

From "SOUTH PACIFIC"

THERE IS NOTHIN' LIKE A DAME

Lyrics by **OSCAR HAMMERSTEIN II**

Music by **RICHARD RODGERS**

We got sun-light on the sand, We got moon-light on the sea, We got man-goes and ba-na-nas You can pick right off a tree, We got vol-ley ball and ping pong And a lot of dan-dy games! What ain't we got? We ain't got dames! We get

From "OLIVER"

AS LONG AS HE NEEDS ME

Words and Music by
LIONEL BART

Chorus, Slowly

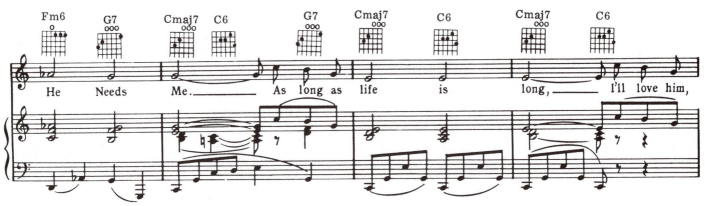

From "FIDDLER ON THE ROOF"

IF I WERE A RICH MAN

Lyrics by **SHELDON HARNICK**

Music by **JERRY BOCK**

bid-dy, bid-dy rich,   dig-guh, dig-guh, dee-dle dai-dle man. I'd build a

big tall house with rooms by the doz-en, Right in the mid-dle of the town;   A

fine tin roof with real wood-en floors be-low.   There could be

one long stair-case just go-ing up and one e-ven long-er com-ing down;   And

From "YOUTH ON PARADE"

I'VE HEARD THAT SONG BEFORE

Lyric by SAMMY CAHN

Music by JULE STYNE

From "HIGH SOCIETY"

TRUE LOVE

Words and Music by
COLE PORTER

From: "MY FAIR LADY"

WITH A LITTLE BIT OF LUCK

Lyrics by ALAN JAY LERNER

Music by FREDERICK LOEWE

From: "BABES IN ARMS"

THE LADY IS A TRAMP

Words by **LORENZ HART**

Music by **RICHARD RODGERS**

From "CINDERELLA"

DO I LOVE YOU
BECAUSE YOU'RE BEAUTIFUL

Words by **OSCAR HAMMERSTEIN II**

Music by **RICHARD RODGERS**

Refrain *(slowly, with warm expression)*

Do I love you be-cause you're beau-ti-ful? Or are you beau-ti-ful be-cause I love you?

From "SOUTH PACIFIC"

A COCK-EYED OPTIMIST

Lyrics by **OSCAR HAMMERSTEIN II**

Music by **RICHARD RODGERS**

From "OKLAHOMA"

OKLAHOMA

Lyrics by **OSCAR HAMMERSTEIN II**

Music by **RICHARD RODGERS**

From "ALL AMERICAN"

ONCE UPON A TIME

Lyric by LEE ADAMS

Music by CHARLES STROUSE

From: "SHALL WE DANCE"

THEY ALL LAUGHED

Lyrics by IRA GERSHWIN

Music by GEORGE GERSHWIN

Refrain *(happily)*

They all laughed at Chris-to-pher Co-lum-bus When he said the World was round.
They all laughed at Rock-e-fel-ler Cen-ter Now they're fight-ing to get in.

They all laughed when Ed-i-son re-cord-ed sound.
They all laughed at Whit-ney and his cot-ton gin.

They all laughed at
They all laughed at

Wil-bur and his broth-er, When they said that man could fly.
Ful-ton and his steam-boat, Her-shey and his choc'-late bar.

From "KISMET"

AND THIS IS MY BELOVED

Words and Music by
ROBERT WRIGHT and
GEORGE FORREST

From "DRAT! THE CAT!"

SHE TOUCHED ME

Lyric by **IRA LEVIN**

Music by **MILTON SCHAFER**

From: "SUNNY SIDE UP"

SUNNY SIDE UP

Words and Music by
B.G. DeSYLVA, LEW BROWN
and **RAY HENDERSON**

From "SITTING PRETTY"

DID YOU EVER SEE A DREAM WALKING?

Words by **MACK GORDON**

Music by **HARRY REVEL**

From "THE BARKLEYS OF BROADWAY"

THEY CAN'T TAKE THAT AWAY FROM ME

Words by **IRA GERSHWIN**

Music by **GEORGE GERSHWIN**

182

From: "GEORGE WHITE'S SCANDALS"

THE THRILL IS GONE

Words and Music by **LEW BROWN**
and **RAY HENDERSON**

From "FINIAN'S RAINBOW"

LOOK TO THE RAINBOW

Lyric by E.Y. HARBURG

Music by BURTON LANE

1. On the day I was born, said my fa - ther, said
2. ('Twas a) sump - tu - ous gift to be - queath to a
3. (So I) bund - led me heart and I roamed the world

he, I've an el - e - gant leg - a - cy
child, Oh the lure of that song kept her
free, To the east with the lark, to the

waitin' for ye, 'Tis a rhyme for your
feet runnin' wild. For you never grow
west with the sea; And I searched all the

lips _____ and a song for your heart, ___ To
old _____ and you never stand still, ___ With
earth _____ and I scanned all the skies, ___ But I

sing it whenever the world falls apart.
whip-poor-wills singin' beyond the next hill.
found it at last in my own true love's eyes.

Look, look, Look to the Rainbow, Follow it

From: "SINCE YOU WENT AWAY"

TOGETHER

Words and Music by
B.G. DeSYLVA, LEW BROWN
and RAY HENDERSON

From "FLOWER DRUM SONG"

I ENJOY BEING A GIRL

Lyrics by **OSCAR HAMMERSTEIN II**

Music by **RICHARD RODGERS**

From "RIGHT THIS WAY"

I CAN DREAM, CAN'T I?

Music by SAMMY FAIN
Words by IRVING KAHAL

From "KNICKERBOCKER HOLIDAY"

SEPTEMBER SONG

Words by **MAXWELL ANDERSON**

Music by **KURT WEILL**

From "PAL JOEY"

BEWITCHED

Words by **LORENZ HART**　　　　　　　　Music by **RICHARD RODGERS**

From "SOUTH PACIFIC"

THIS NEARLY WAS MINE

Lyrics by **OSCAR HAMMERSTEIN II**

Music by **RICHARD RODGERS**

208

Still say-ing that par-a-dise _____ Once near-ly was mine.

mine. _____ mine. _____ mine. So

clear and deep are my fan-cies _____ Of things I

wish _ were true. _____ I'll keep re-mem-b'ring

From "GYPSY"

SMALL WORLD

Words by **STEPHEN SONDHEIM**

Music by **JULE STYNE**

stran - ger my - self here. Small world, is - n't it?

Fun - ny, — you're a {girl man} who goes trav' - ling, Rath - er than set - tling

down. Fun - ny, — 'cause I'd love to go trav' - ling.

Small world, is - n't it? We have

so much in com-mon, It's a phe-nom-e-non. We could pool our re-sourc-es by join-ing forc-es from now on.— Luck-y,— you're a {girl}{man} who likes chil-dren, That's an im-por-tant sign.

From: "FINIAN'S RAINBOW"

WHEN I'M NOT NEAR THE GIRL I LOVE

Words by E.Y. HARBURG

Music by BURTON LANE

From: "SUNNY SIDE UP"

IF I HAD A TALKING PICTURE OF YOU

Words and Music by
B.G. DeSYLVA, LEW BROWN
and RAY HENDERSON

From "SONG OF NORWAY"

STRANGE MUSIC

From "WEDDING DAY IN TROLDHAUGEN"
by: EDVARD GRIEG

Words and Music by
ROBERT WRIGHT
GEORGE FORREST

From "BABES IN ARMS"

I WISH I WERE IN LOVE AGAIN

Lyrics by **LORENZ HART**

Music by **RICHARD RODGERS**

From: "GIGI"

THE NIGHT THEY INVENTED CHAMPAGNE

Lyrics by **ALAN JAY LERNER**

Music by **FREDERICK LOEWE**

From "A DAMSEL IN DISTRESS"

NICE WORK IF YOU CAN GET IT

Words by **IRA GERSHWIN**

Music by **GEORGE GERSHWIN**

Where two hearts be-come one_ Who could ask for an-y-thing more?

Lov-ing one who loves you, And then tak-ing that vow,

Nice work if you can get it, And if you get it,_ Won't you tell me

how?

how?

From "PARIS"

LET'S DO IT

(LET'S FALL IN LOVE)

Words and Music by
COLE PORTER

235

From: "LOVE ME TONIGHT"

LOVER

Words by **LORENZ HART**

Music by **RICHARD RODGERS**

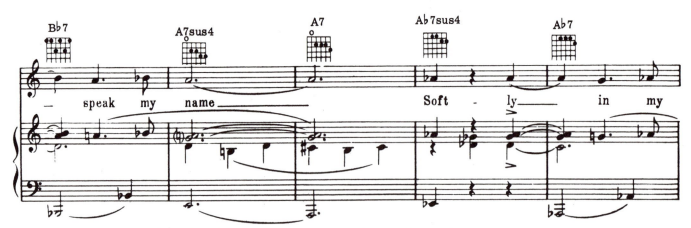

From "LADY BE GOOD"

OH, LADY BE GOOD!

Words by **IRA GERSHWIN**

Music by **GEORGE GERSHWIN**

* Diagrams for Guitar, Symbols for
Ukulele and Banjo

From "MILK AND HONEY"

SHALOM

Words and Music by
JERRY HERMAN

Fine

when you say good-bye, you say good - bye with SHA - LOM.____

Interlude

It's a ver-y use - ful word,____ It can get you through the day;____

All you real-ly need to know,____ You can hard-ly go wrong, this is

D. C. al Fine

your home as long as you say:_____ SHA

From: "THE BEST THINGS IN LIFE ARE FREE"

BUTTON UP YOUR OVERCOAT

Words and Music by
B.G. DeSYLVA, LEW BROWN
and **RAY HENDERSON**

But-ton up your o-ver-coat_ When the wind is free
But-ton up your o-ver-coat_ When the wind is free

Take good_ care of your-self_ you be-long to me! _
Take good_ care of your-self_ you be-long to me! _

Eat an ap-ple ev-'ry day;_ Get to bed by three
Wear your flan-nel un-der-wear_ When you climb a tree

Take good_ care of your-self_ you be-long to me! _ Be care-ful
Take good_ care of your-self_ you be-long to me! _ Don't sit on

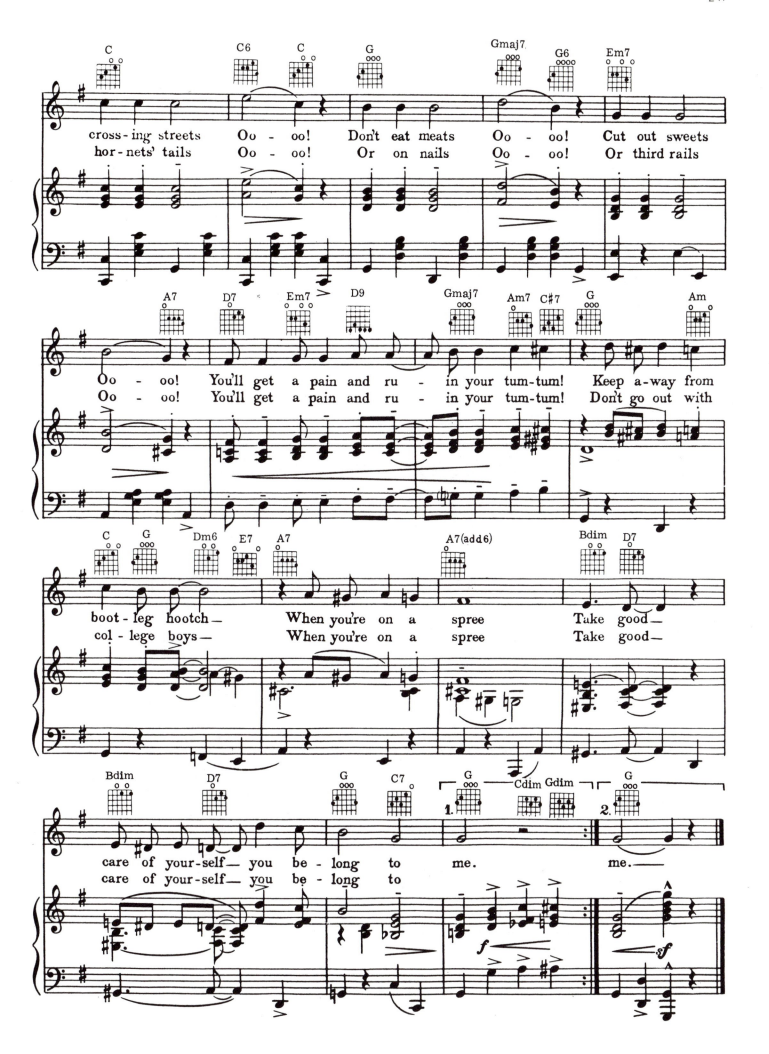

From: "PALE FACE"

BUTTONS AND BOWS

Words and Music by
JAY LIVINGSTON and
RAY EVANS

From "ON A CLEAR DAY YOU CAN SEE FOREVER"

ON A CLEAR DAY

(YOU CAN SEE FOREVER)

Words by **ALAN JAY LERNER**   Music by **BURTON LANE**

From: "GOLDWYN FOLLIES"

LOVE WALKED IN

Words by IRA GERSHWIN

Music by GEORGE GERSHWIN

world com-plete-ly new, When love walked in with

you. you.

From: "PAL JOEY"

I COULD WRITE A BOOK

Words by **LORENZ HART**   Music by **RICHARD RODGERS**

Slowly

If they asked me I could write a book,

A - bout the way you walk and whis - per and

From: "CAMELOT"

HOW TO HANDLE A WOMAN

Music by **FREDERICK LOEWE**

Lyrics by **ALAN JAY LERNER**

way to han-dle a wom-an is to love her,_____

Sim-ply love her,_____ Mere-ly

love her, love her, love her!"_____

love her!"

From "THE SOUND OF MUSIC"
THE SOUND OF MUSIC

Words by **OSCAR HAMMERSTEIN II**

Music by **RICHARD RODGERS**

Refrain *(moderately, with warm expression)*

mu - sic. My heart wants to sing ev - 'ry song it

hears. My heart wants to beat like the wings of the

birds that rise from the lake to the trees. My

heart wants to sigh like a chime that flies from a church on a

From: "GEORGE WHITE'S SCANDALS"

LIFE IS JUST A BOWL OF CHERRIES

Words and Music by **LEW BROWN**
and **RAY HENDERSON**

From: "LEAVE IT TO ME"

MY HEART BELONGS TO DADDY

Words and Music by
COLE PORTER

swell, That my heart be-longs_ to Dad-dy__ 'Cause my

Dad-dy, he treats it so well. While well.

From: "TWO FOR THE SHOW"

HOW HIGH THE MOON

Words by NANCY HAMILTON   **Music by MORGAN LEWIS**

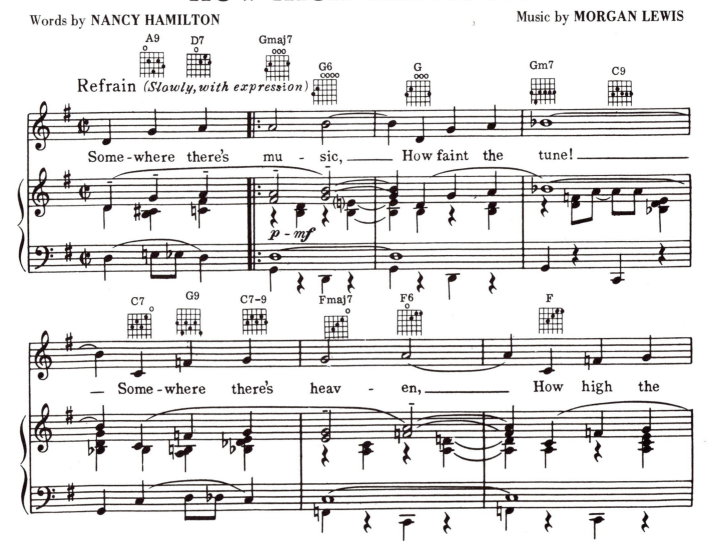

Refrain *(Slowly, with expression)*

Some-where there's mu-sic, ____ How faint the tune! ____

__ Some-where there's heav - en, _____ How high the

From: "THE DESERT SONG"

THE DESERT SONG

Lyrics by **OTTO HARBACH & OSCAR HAMMERSTEIN II**

Music by **SIGMUND ROMBERG**

From: "THE DESERT SONG"

ONE ALONE

Lyrics by **OTTO HARBACH & OSCAR HAMMERSTEIN II**

Music by **SIGMUND ROMBERG**

From: "MY FAIR LADY"

THE RAIN IN SPAIN

Lyrics by **ALAN JAY LERNER**

Music by **FREDERICK LOEWE**

From "ROSE-MARIE"

ROSE-MARIE

Lyrics by **OTTO HARBACH & OSCAR HAMMERSTEIN II**

Music by **RUDOLF FRIML**

From "THE NEW MOON"

WANTING YOU

Lyrics by OSCAR HAMMERSTEIN II

Music by SIGMUND ROMBERG

long - ing to _____ Hold you close to my ea - ger breast;

Want - ing love, ___ in that heav- en I'm dream-ing of ___ Makes that heav - en seem

far a - bove ___ An - v hope that I'll gain my quest. ___

espressivo

Dreams are vain, _____ But I cling to the mer - est

From "THE NEW MOON"

LOVER, COME BACK TO ME!

Lyrics by **OSCAR HAMMERSTEIN II**

Music by **SIGMUND ROMBERG**

walked a-long with you, No won-der I am lone - ly.

The sky is blue, The night is cold, The moon is new,

But love is old, And, while I'm wait-ing here, This heart of mine is sing-ing:

"Lov - er come back to me!" me!"

From "A CONNECTICUT YANKEE"

MY HEART STOOD STILL

Lyrics by **LORENZ HART**

Music by **RICHARD RODGERS**

REFRAIN
Slow, but liltingly

I took one look at you, That's all I meant to do;

And then my heart stood still!

My feet could step and walk, My lips could move and talk,

And yet my heart stood still! Though not a

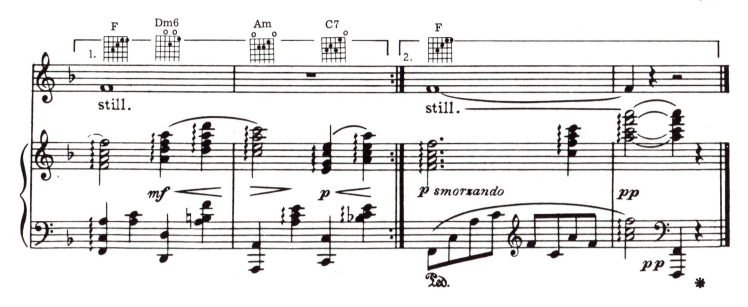

From "PRESENT ARMS"

YOU TOOK ADVANTAGE OF ME

Lyrics by **LORENZ HART**

Music by **RICHARD RODGERS**

From "GARRICK GAIETIES"

MANHATTAN

Lyrics by **LORENZ HART**

Music by **RICHARD RODGERS**

From "HOLD EVERYTHING"

YOU'RE THE CREAM IN MY COFFEE

Words and Music by
B.G. DeSYLVA, LEW BROWN
and **RAY HENDERSON**

From "LOVE ME TONIGHT"

MIMI

Words by **LORENZ HART**

Music by **RICHARD RODGERS**

From: "KILL THAT STORY"

TWO CIGARETTES IN THE DARK

Lyric by **PAUL FRANCIS WEBSTER**   Music by **LEW POLLACK**

From "WE'RE NOT DRESSING"

LOVE THY NEIGHBOR

Words by **MACK GORDON**

Music by **HARRY REVEL**

From "LOVE ME TONIGHT"

ISN'T IT ROMANTIC

Words and Music by
LORENZ HART and
RICHARD RODGERS

From: "BABES IN ARMS"

WHERE OR WHEN

Lyrics by **LORENZ HART** Music by **RICHARD RODGERS**

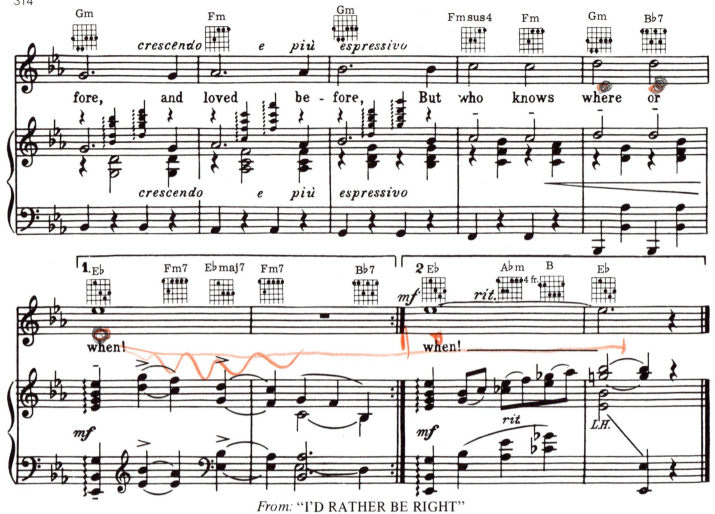

From: "I'D RATHER BE RIGHT"

HAVE YOU MET MISS JONES

Lyrics by **LORENZ HART**   Music by **RICHARD RODGERS**

From: "PARIS IN THE SPRING"

PARIS IN THE SPRING

Lyric and Music by
MACK GORDON
HARRY REVEL

* *Diagrams for Guitar Accomp.*

From "ZIEGFELD FOLLIES: 1936"

I CAN'T GET STARTED

Words by **IRA GERSHWIN**

Music by **VERNON DUKE**

From "FUNNY GIRL"

PEOPLE

Words by **BOB MERRILL**

Music by **JULE STYNE**

From: "SUNNY SIDE UP"

(I'M A DREAMER)
AREN'T WE ALL?

Words and Music by
**B.G. DeSYLVA, LEW BROWN
and RAY HENDERSON**

From "GEORGE WHITE'S SCANDALS"

THE BIRTH OF THE BLUES

Words by
B. G. DE SYLVA
and LEW BROWN
A.S.C.A.P.

Music by
RAY HENDERSON
A.S.C.A.P.

*Diagrams for Guitar, Symbols for
Ukulele and Banjo

© MCMXXVI by HARMS, INC.
Copyright renewed

PUBLISHED BY ARRANGEMENT WITH ROSS JUNGNICKEL INC

From "INNOCENTS OF PARIS"

LOUISE

Words by **LEO ROBIN**

Music by **RICHARD A. WHITING**

From "LADY BE GOOD"

FASCINATING RHYTHM

Words by
IRA GERSHWIN

Music by
GEORGE GERSHWIN

"Fas-ci-nat-ing Rhy-thm You've got me on the go! Fas-ci - nat-ing Rhy-thm I'm all a-

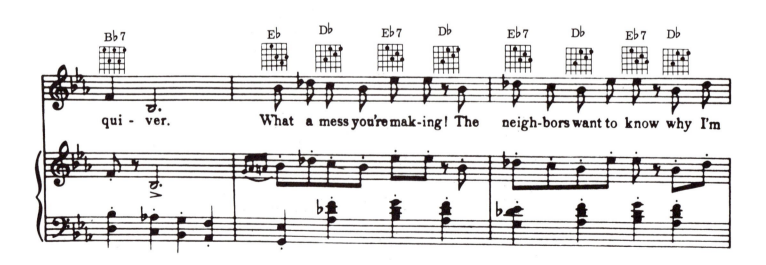

qui - ver. What a mess you're mak-ing! The neigh-bors want to know why I'm

From: "CENTENNIAL SUMMER"

ALL THROUGH THE DAY

Lyrics by OSCAR HAMMERSTEIN II

Music by JEROME KERN

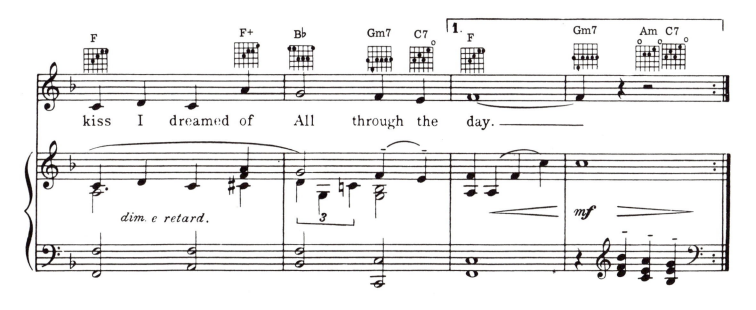

kiss I dreamed of All through the day. ____

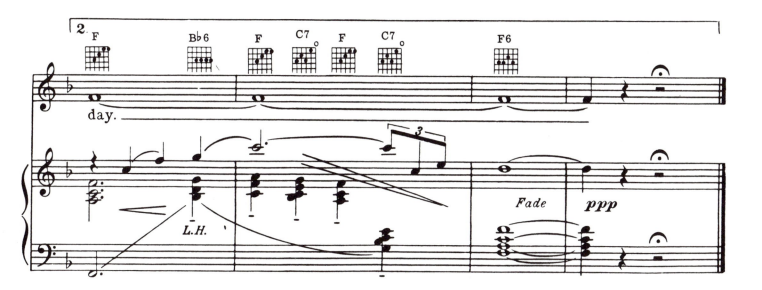

day. ____

From: "CAN–CAN"

ALLEZ-VOUS-EN, GO AWAY

Music and Lyrics by
COLE PORTER

Refrain *(Slow Valse tempo with much expression)*

Al - lez-vous - en,*____ al - lez-vous - en,____ {Mam' - selle,
{M' - sieur,

legato

*Pronounce: Al-lay-voo-zon
(French for Go away.)

From: "BYE BYE BIRDIE"

A LOT OF LIVIN' TO DO

Lyric by **LEE ADAMS**

Music by **CHARLES STROUSE**

345

From "BITTER SWEET"

ZIGEUNER

Words and Music by
NOEL COWARD

tor-tur-ing her so.___ Then a gyp-sy came, Called to her by

name, Woo'd her with a song Sen-su-ous and strong. All the sum-mer

long Her pas-sion seemed to trem-ble like a liv-ing frame.

REFRAIN

Play to me be-neath the sum-mer moon, Zi - geu - -

From "SOMETHING TO SHOUT ABOUT"

YOU'D BE SO NICE TO COME HOME TO

Words and Music by
COLE PORTER

Allegretto comodo

It's not that you're fair-er, Than a lot of girls just as pleas-in', That I doff my hat as a wor-ship-per at your shrine,— It's

From "PROMISES, PROMISES"
PROMISES, PROMISES

Lyric by **HAL DAVID**

Music by **BURT BACHARACH**

From "OF THEE I SING"

WHO CARES?

(So Long As You Care For Me)

Words by **IRA GERSHWIN**   Music by **GEORGE GERSHWIN**

From "THE MUSIC MAN"

SEVENTY SIX TROMBONES

Words and Music by
MEREDITH WILLSON

Thun-der-ing, thun-der-ing, loud-er than be-fore. Clar-i nets of

ev-'ry size and trum-pet-ers who'd im-pro-vise a full oc-tave high-er than the

score.

Sev-en-ty Six Trom - bones led the big pa-rade,____ When the or-der to

364

one and on-ly bass, And I oom-pahed up and down the square.____

A la Tuba

Buh buh buh buh buh buh buh buh buh buh buh,____ Buh buh buh buh buh

buh buh buh buh buh buh.____ Buh buh buh buh buh

buh buh buh buh buh buh buh buh buh buh

buh ___ buh buh buh buh buh buh. ___

Sev - en - ty Six Trom - bones hit the coun - ter - point, ___

___ While a hun - dred and ten cor - nets played the air. ___

___ Then I mod - est - ly took my place as the one and on - ly

bass, And I oom - pahed, oom - pahed, oom - pah - pahed,

oom - pahed up and down the square. Sev - en - ty

square.

From "PRIVATE LIVES"

SOMEDAY I'LL FIND YOU

Words and Music by
NOËL COWARD

Some-day I'll find you, Moon-light be-hind you, True to the dream I am dream - ing. As I draw near you You'll smile a lit-tle smile; For a lit-tle while We shall stand Hand in hand. I'll leave you

From "MEXICAN HAYRIDE"
I LOVE YOU

Music and Lyrics by
COLE PORTER

From "BETWEEN THE DEVIL"

I SEE YOUR FACE BEFORE ME

Lyrics by **HOWARD DIETZ**

Music by **ARTHUR SCHWARTZ**

From "THUMBS UP"

ZING! WENT THE STRINGS OF MY HEART

Words and Music by
JAMES F. HANLEY

Nev - er could car - ry a tune, Nev - er knew where to start, You

came a - long when ev - 'ry-thing was wrong And put a song in my heart.

Dear, when you smiled at me I heard a mel - o - dy,

378

p a tempo

I still re-call the thrill, I guess I al-ways will,__ I hope 'twill

nev-er de-part, _____ Dear, with your

lips to mine __ A rhap-so-dy di-vine.__ Zing! went the

strings of my heart. heart._____

8va bassa

From "ST. LOUIS WOMAN"

ANY PLACE I HANG MY HAT IS HOME

Words by **JOHNNY MERCER**

Music by **HAROLD ARLEN**

From "PICKWICK"

IF I RULED THE WORLD

Words by **LESLIE BRICUSSE**

Music by **CYRIL ORNADEL**

385

From "DUBARRY WAS A LADY"

FRIENDSHIP

Words and Music by
COLE PORTER

From: "LEAVE IT TO ME"

GET OUT OF TOWN

Words and Music by
COLE PORTER

Names of chords for Ukulele and Banjo.
Symbols for Guitar.

From "LADY BE GOOD"

THE MAN I LOVE

Words by IRA GERSHWIN
French version by Emilia Renaud
Spanish text by Johnny Camacho

Music by GEORGE GERSHWIN

From "A STAR IS BORN"

THE MAN THAT GOT AWAY

(THE GAL THAT GOT AWAY)

Lyric by **IRA GERSHWIN**

Music by **HAROLD ARLEN**

From "ROSE-MARIE"

INDIAN LOVE CALL

Words by
OTTO HARBACH and
OSCAR HAMMERSTEIN II

Music by
RUDOLF FRIML

Refrain *(slowly) con molto sentimento*

you __ oo - oo __ oo - oo - oo! __ Will you an-swer

too __ oo - oo __ oo - oo - oo? __

That means I of - fer my love to you __ to be your own. __

If you re - fuse me, I will be blue __ And wait - ing

Song Listing of Broadway Shows

All American
Once Upon A Time

Babes In Arms
I Wish I Were In Love Again
Where Or When
The Lady Is A Tramp

The Barkleys Of Broadway
They Can't Take That Away From Me

Bells Are Ringing
Long Before I Knew You

(The) Best Things In Life Are Free
Button Up Your Overcoat

Between The Devil
I See Your Face Before Me

Bitter Sweet
Zigeuner

Born To Dance
I've Got You Under My Skin

Bye Bye Birdie
A Lot Of Livin' To Do

Camelot
How To Handle A Woman

Can-Can
Allez-Vous-En, Go Away
C'est Magnifique

Centennial Summer
All Through The Day

Cinderella
Do I Love You Because You're Beautiful

(A) Connecticut Yankee
My Heart Stood Still

(A) Damsel In Distress
A Foggy Day
Nice Work If You Can Get It

Desert Song
The Desert Song
One Alone

Drat! The Cat!
She Touched Me

Dubarry Was A Lady
Do I Love You?
Friendship

Fiddler On The Roof
If I Were A Rich Man

Finian's Rainbow
Look To The Rainbow
When I'm Not Near The Girl I Love

Flower Drum Song
I Enjoy Being A Girl

Funny Girl
People

Garrick Gaieties
Manhattan

George White's Scandals
The Thrill Is Gone
Life Is Just A Bowl Of Cherries
The Birth Of The Blues

Gigi
Thank Heaven For Little Girls
(The) Night They Invented Champagne

Goldwyn Follies
Love Walked In

Good News
Lucky In Love

Guys And Dolls
Luck Be A Lady

Gypsy
Small World

Hello Dolly
It Only Takes A Moment

High Society
True Love

Hold Everything
You're The Cream In My Coffee

I Do, I Do
My Cup Runneth Over

I'd Rather Be Right
Have You Met Miss Jones

Innocents Of Paris
Louise

Keeps Rainin' All The Time
Stormy Weather

Kill That Story
Two Cigarettes In The Dark

Kismet
Stranger In Paradise
And This Is My Beloved
Baubles Bangles And Beads

Knickerbocker Holiday
September Song

Lady Be Good
Oh, Lady Be Good
The Man I Love
Fascinating Rhythm

Leave It To Me
My Heart Belongs To Daddy
Get Out Of Town

Les Girls
Ca, C'est L'amour

Love Me Tonight
Isn't It Romantic
Lover
Mimi

Me And Juliet
No Other Love

Mexican Hayride
I Love You

Milk And Honey
Shalom

The Music Man
Seventy-Six Trombones
Till There Was You

My Fair Lady
I've Grown Accustomed To Her Face
The Rain In Spain
Wouldn't It Be Loverly
On The Street Where You Live
With A Little Bit Of Luck

The New Moon
Wanting You
Lover Come Back To Me!

The New Yorkers
Love For Sale

No Strings
The Sweetest Sounds

Of Thee I Sing
Who Cares (So Long As You Care For Me)

Oklahoma
Oklahoma

Oliver
As Long As He Needs Me

On A Clear Day (You Can See Forever)

On A Clear Day (You Can See Forever)

One Touch Of Venus

Speak Low

Out Of This World

From This Moment On

Pale Face

Buttons And Bows

Pal Joey

Bewitched

I Could Write A Book

Paris

Let's Do It (Let's Fall In Love)

Paris In The Spring

Paris In The Spring

Pickwick

If I Ruled The World

Porgy And Bess

It Ain't Necessarily So

Present Arms

You Took Advantage Of Me

Private Lives

Someday I'll Find You

Promises, Promises

Promises, Promises

I'll Never Fall In Love Again

Right This Way

I Can Dream Can't I

Rose-Marie

Indian Love Call

Rose-Marie

Shall We Dance

They all Laughed

Shuffle Along
I'm Just Wild About Harry

Since You Went Away
Together

Sitting Pretty
Did You Ever See A Dream Walking?

Something To Shout About
You'd Be So Nice To Come Home To

Song Of Norway
Strange Music

The Sound Of Music
The Sound Of Music

South Pacific
A Cock-eyed Optimist
Happy Talk
There Is Nothin' Like A Dame
This Nearly Was Mine

A Star Is Born
The Man That Got Away

St. Louis Woman
Come Rain Or Come Shine
Any Place I Hang My Hat Is Home

Stop The World — I Want To Get Off
Gonna Build A Mountain

Sunny Side Up
Sunny Side Up
(I'm A Dreamer) Aren't We All?
If I Had A Talking Picture Of You

Thumbs Up
Zing! Went The Strings Of My Heart

Two For The Show
How High The Moon